THE PORTABLE 7 HABITS™

Purpose

Focusing on What Matters Most

THE 7 HABITS
OF HIGHLY EFFECTIVE PEOPLE®

Other Portable 7 Habits Books
Choice: Choosing the Proactive Life You Want to Live
Vision: Defining Your Destiny in Life
Abundance: Fulfilling Your Potential for Success
Trust: Sharing Ideas, Insights, and Understanding
Synergy: Connecting to the Power of Cooperation
Renewal: Nourishing Body, Mind, Heart, and Soul

Other Books from Franklin Covey
The 7 Habits of Highly Effective People
The 7 Habits of Highly Effective Families
The 7 Habits of Highly Effective Teens
The 7 Habits of Highly Effective Teens Journal
Daily Reflections for Highly Effective Teens
Daily Reflections for Highly Effective People
Living the 7 Habits

Loving Reminders for Kids
Loving Reminders for Couples
Loving Reminders for Families
Loving Reminders Teen to Teen
Loving Reminders to Make Kids Laugh
Quotes and Quips

Franklin Covey
2200 West Parkway Boulevard
Salt Lake City, Utah 84119-2099

Concept: Cheryl Kerzner
Design: Jenny Peterson
Illustration: Tammy Smith
Written and compiled by Debra Harris
Contributors: John Crowley, Ann Hobson, Sunny Larson, Shelley Orgill

Manufactured in United States of America

ISBN 1-929494-11-4

CONTENTS

Each day has its own purpose and fits into the great plan of our life. This very moment carries traces of our life purpose in places where we focus our attention, in words or ideas that bring a tingle of excitement and hope in our heart.

—CAROL ADRIENNE

INTRODUCTION

In order to live a more balanced existence, you have to recognize that not doing everything that comes your way is OK. There's no need to overextend yourself anymore. All it takes is realizing that it's alright to say "no" when need be. And prioritizing what matters most. But before you can move ahead you need to become clear about who you are and what you really want.

In *Purpose: Focusing on What Matters Most*, we've simplified the powerful principles behind *The 7 Habits of Highly Effective People* by Stephen R. Covey to help you reconnect with what's most important in your life.

There are no roadmaps to follow. No instructions. No how-tos. And no formulas for success. Instead you'll find a collection of contemporary quotes, thought-provoking questions, provocative messages, and practical wisdom in an easy-to-read format.

As you turn these pages, take the words of advice to heart, mind, body, and soul. Think about what you read. Ponder how and what it would take to manage your life more effectively. Let the wisdom inspire you to redefine your priorities and create more time for the most important things. Which means clearing out the clutter and peeling back the layers to rediscover what you really care about.

In essence, make it a habit to focus on what matters most.

HABIT 3: PUT FIRST THINGS FIRST®

Prioritize, and do the most important things first.

PURPOSE

An effective goal focuses primarily on results rather than activity. It identifies where you want to be, and in the process helps you determine where you are. It gives you important information on how to get there, and it tells you when you have arrived. It unifies your efforts or energy. It gives meaning and purpose to all you do.

—STEPHEN R. COVEY, *The 7 Habits of Highly Effective People*

THIS LIFE IS A TEST.

It is only a test. If this were an actual life, you would have been given further instructions and told where to go and what to do.

—ANONYMOUS

The purpose
of our lives
is to give
birth to the
best which
is within us.

—MARIANNE WILLIAMSON

RAISE THE BAR.

*L*ike most of us humans (if you're a nonhuman and are another species of animal instead like a llama, screechmonkey, or whatever, then congratulations on learning how to read), I am always searching for answers. Sometimes I don't even know the question, and yet I need answers. Sometimes I know the answer and I need the question, but that's only when I'm watching *Jeopardy*.

—ELLEN DEGENERES

Sometimes in your life you will go on a journey. It will be the longest journey you have ever taken. It is the journey to find yourself.

—KATHERINE SHARP

What little issues are blocking your energy?

Where will your journey take you?

Once you begin the journey
toward a life of purpose, you **enter the realm of
real magic.**

—WAYNE DYER

G E T   C L E A R   A B O U T
YOUR LIFE PURPOSE

➤ Ask yourself if you really want to pursue and follow your purpose.

➤ Listen to your inner voice to guide you along the path.

➤ Figure out what is working and what isn't working in your life.

➤ Look at what you want to change about your life.

➤ Make small changes instead of trying to take on everything at once.

➤ Create realistic goals and strategies.

➤ Forget about what others think of your desire to change.

➤ Believe that anything is possible when you're on purpose.

➤ Realize everything happens for a reason when it is supposed to happen.

➤ Create accountability for your progress toward your life's purpose.

➤ Always remember it is up to you to make it or break it.

When you are inspired by some great purpose, some extraordinary projects, all your thoughts break their bonds; your mind transcends limitations; your consciousness expands in every direction; and you find yourself in a great new and wonderful world. Dormant forces, faculties and talents become alive and you discover yourself to be a greater person by far than you ever dreamed yourself to be.

—PATANJALI

Own what you think and feel.

VALUES

You are a disciple, a follower, of your own deep values and their source. And you have the will, the integrity, to subordinate your feelings, your impulses, your moods to those values.

—STEPHEN R. COVEY, The 7 Habits of Highly Effective People

If you seek what is **HONORABLE**, what is **GOOD**, what is **THE TRUTH** of your life, all the other things you could not imagine come as a matter of course.

—OPRAH WINFREY

There are many things in life that will catch your eye, but only a few will catch your heart.

Pursue them.

—ANONYMOUS

Without taking a lot of time, answer the following

questions and think about what comes to mind.

Explore any reccuring theme.

What **values** are most important to you?

What **interests** you most?

What do you feel **passionate** about?

What is **important** to you?

What do you want to **accomplish**?

What do you want to **contribute**?

What do you **believe** in?

What is your **potential**?

What are your **strengths**?

What do you **stand** for?

Believing in something makes it possible.

It doesn't necessarily make it easy.

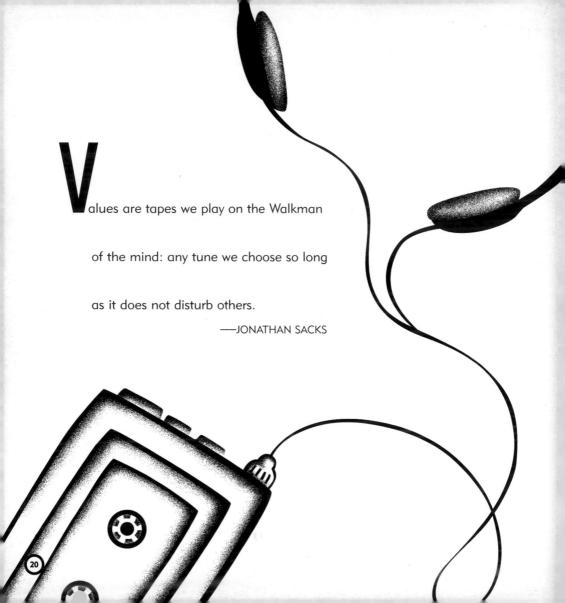

Values are tapes we play on the Walkman

of the mind: any tune we choose so long

as it does not disturb others.

—JONATHAN SACKS

20

Are you

still STRIVING

still DREAMING

still CHANGING

still BECOMING

still DOING

?????

The trouble with many of us is that we just slide along in life. If we would only give, just once, the same amount of reflection to what we want out of life that we give to the question of what to do with a two weeks' vacation, we would be startled at our false standards and the aimless procession of our busy days.

—DOROTHY CANFIELD FISHER

A wise man on my way

once taught me that

it is not important to arrive first, but to know

how to arrive.

—UNKNOWN

Do you Live what you Believe?

Let me ask you something—
if someone's really lying,
are their pants really on fire?

—JERRY SEINFELD

Might be and might have been will become what is if you worry about it.

ROLES

Writing your mission in terms of the important roles in your life gives you balance and harmony. It keeps each role clearly before you. You can review your roles frequently to make sure that you don't get totally absorbed by one role to the exclusion of the others that are equally or even more important in your life.

——STEPHEN R. COVEY, *The 7 Habits of Highly Effective People*

partner

social icon

leader

fun fanatic

parent

worker bee

boss

downtown diva

guru-of-the-moment

mentor

friend

volunteer

WHAT ARE YOUR ROLES?

pity princess

teacher

advocate

fashion police

superwoman

creator

Martha Stewart wannabe

multitasker

boy wonder

student

sports hero

drama queen

king of the world

There are as many ways to live and grow as there are people. Our own ways are the only ways that should matter to us.

—EVELYN MANDEL

There's a
STAR
in every one of us.

BE
SIGNIFICANT.

No sooner do we think we have assembled a comfortable life

than we find a piece of ourselves that has no place to fit in.

—GAIL SHEEHY

I know you are, but but What am I?

—PEE WEE HERMAN

I am not the victim of the world I see.

I have invented the world I see.

—A COURSE IN MIRACLES

The important thing is this:

to be able at any moment to sacrifice what we are for what we

could become.

—CHARLES DUBOIS

There comes a point in many people's lives when they can no longer play the role they have chosen for themselves. When that happens, we are like actors finding that someone has changed the play.

—BRIAN MOORE

Every game we play,
we slip into a role,
a game identity with which to play.

We decide whether we're the rescuer, victim,

leader-with-all-the-answers, followers-without-

a-clue, bright, brave, honorable, crafty, dull,

helpless, just-trying-to-get-along, diabolical,

easy-going, pitiable, earnest, careless, salt-of-

the-earth, puppetmaster, comic, hero...we

choose our role by whim and destiny, and

we can change it anytime we want.

—RICHARD BACH

It's never too late to become the real you.

PRIORITIES

The key is not to prioritize what's on your schedule, but to schedule your priorities.

—STEPHEN R. COVEY, *The 7 Habits of Highly Effective People*

When your heart is in your dream,
no request is too extreme.

—JIMINY CRICKET

Remember,

no agenda or problem is more profound than your own.

—JANEANE GAROFALO

1 · 2 · 3 · 4 · 5

What are your

TOP FIVE

priorities that need the most attention?

We have to find ways to **exercise the compassion of our hearts,** and at the same moment learn how to know what the limits are and be able to say no without guilt.

—RAM DASS

POWER LOUNGING

isn't an option.

I tried to teach my child with books.

He gave me only puzzled looks.

I tried to teach my child with words.

They passed him by often unheard.

Despairingly, I turned aside,

"How shall I teach this child?" I cried.

"Come," he said, *"Play with me!"*

—ANONYMOUS

45

Opportunities are never lost; they're just found by someone else.

When we are capable of stopping, we begin to see.
——THICH NHAT NANH

What have you been ignoring that is
calling for your attention?

Perhaps all human progress stems from

the tension between two basic drives:

to have what **everyone** else has

and to have what **no one** has.

—JUDITH STONE

Winners make a life before they make a living.

COMMITMENT

Keep in mind that you are always saying "no" to something. It it isn't to the apparent, urgent things in your life, it is probably to the more fundamental, highly important things. Even if the urgent is good, the good can keep you from your best, keep you from your unique contribution, if you let it.

—STEPHEN R. COVEY, *The 7 Habits of Highly Effective People*

It's great to be a

BIG TIME

thinker as long as you're a big time

DOER.

At some level,

we too, have to **make an ultimate sacrifice** to our

callings. We need to devote everything, our whole

selves. A part-time effort, a sorta-kinda commitment,

an untested promise, won't suffice. You must know

that you mean business, that you're going to jump

into it up to your eye sockets and not turn back at

the last minute.

—GREGG LEVOY

The thing is to stalk your calling in a certain skilled and supple way to locate the most tender and live spot and plug into the pulse.

—ANNIE DILLARD

Sit, walk or run, but don't wobble.

The greatest thing in this world is not so much where we stand as in what direction we are moving.

—JOHANN WOLFGANG VON GOETHE

T

here is a force that somehow pushes us to

choose the more difficult path whereby we can

transcend the mire and muck into which we are

so often born. Despite all that resists the

process, we do become better human beings.

—M. SCOTT PECK

What you **WILL** do
is what matters,
not what you can do.

$\mathcal{S}$ometimes...when you hold out for everything, you walk away with nothing.

— *ALLY MCBEAL*

You have to know what you want to get, but when you know that, let it take you. And if it seems to take you off the track, don't hold back, because perhaps that is instinctively where you want to be. And if you hold back and try to be always where you have been before, you will go dry.

—GERTRUDE STEIN

PLAN

Happiness can be defined, in part at least, as the fruit of the desire and ability to sacrifice what we want now for what we want eventually.

—STEPHEN R. COVEY, *The 7 Habits of Highly Effective People*

Instant gratification takes too long.

—CARRIE FISHER

You'll **end up** **where you're** **headed** if you don't **watch** **out.**

Tell me, what is it you plan to do with your one wild and precious life? —MARY OLIVER

ARE YOU TOO BUSY

doing what you're doing to write a to-do list?

WHAT'S YOUR
CHAOS QUOTIENT?

- Do you deliberately call people when you know you'll get their answering machines because you don't have time to talk?

- Are you often late paying bills because you forget about them?

- Does the idea of being sick in bed for a day drive you to despair?

- Do you often have trouble putting your hands on a phone number or a memo when you need it?

- Do you have a hard time remembering the last time you had a relaxing lunch with a friend?

- Do your vacation days pile up every year because you don't have time to take them?

- Do you have old magazines and newspapers that are more than a month old that you keep meaning to read?

- Do you ever forget appointments?

- Do you have a hard time saying no when someone asks for a moment of your time?

SCORE: If you answered yes to three or fewer, you're in basically good health. If you a answered yes to between four to six, you need an immediate checkup. If you answered yes to seven or more, emergency CPR is required.

—STEPHANIE WINSTON

If you have no plan
for your life
it won't go
according to plan.

Beingness, doingness and havingness are like a triangle where each side supports the others. They are not in conflict with each other. They all exist simultaneously.

—SHAKTI GAWAIN

RIGHT NOW, THIS MINUTE

WHAT CAN YOU DO TO LIVE A LESS HECTIC LIFE?

The day when we plan seriously to start living either never comes or it comes too late.

——IDA ALEXA ROSS WYLIE

ORGANIZE

As you work to develop a paradigm that empowers you to see through the lens of importance rather than urgency, you will increase your ability to organize and execute every week of your life around your deepest priorities, to walk your talk.

—STEPHEN R. COVEY, *The 7 Habits of Highly Effective People*

It's the start that stops most people.

You May Be on Stuff Overload If...

◆ You have a huge collection of empty plastic margarine containers.

◆ You have junkmail you haven't opened in months.

◆ Your basement Is crammed with boxes from your last move five years ago.

◆ You save every catalog—even the bass fishing one and you don't fish.

◆ You have any of the following sitting around: lamp that needs to be rewired; a picture frame without the glass; a pile of clothes you've been meaning to give away; an old coffee table that you're going to refinish someday.

◆ You have a drawer full of coupons for items you'll never buy.

◆ People call you "Pack Rat" to your face and you think it's a compliment.

◆ You have piles of outdated magazines you still can't part with.

◆ You have junk drawers that you're afraid to open.

DUE TO A MAJOR EMERGENCY,

you've been told you must leave your home immediately.

You can only take what you can fit in your car.

YOU HAVE 5 MINUTES.

What will you take?

Most **urgencies** are simply

other people's priorities.

I'd been busy, busy, so busy, preparing
for life, while life floated by me,
quiet and swift as a regatta.

—LORENE CARY

Next time never comes.

$\mathcal{T}$ime management is really a misnomer—the challenge is not to manage time, but to manage ourselves.

—STEPHEN R. COVEY

DON'T AGONIZE. GET ORGANIZED.

1. When establishing a general storage system, you have four storage choices. You can hang it, put it in a drawer, store it on the floor, or shelve it. If you haven't used it in a year, chances are you never will.

2. Get rid of anything that you haven't used for the past year or two, except tax and business documents. Sorting will reduce your storage needs and save you valuable time and money in the process.

3. Managing paper is a challenge we all face. Consolidate important notes into a daily planner, spiral notebook, large calendar, or wipe off board. Use a multicolored pen or marker to flag special events, with one color per event or person.

4. Create a follow up system using a file box and index cards, or notebook with pocketed dividers.

5. For bills and other correspondence, buy a notebook with twelve pocketed dividers, one for each month of the year. Label each with birthdays, anniversaries, and billing due dates, then fill with correspondence. The binder can be used as a portable desk, or can be stored at your work area.

6. Set a specific day of the month to do your paperwork.

7. Minimize organizing product costs by clipping articles and recipes, then discarding the remainder of the magazine. Store in magnetic photo albums, or a notebook with dividers.

—DEBBIE WILLIAMS

What time would it be if all the clocks were stopped?

—ZEN SAYING

BALANCE

As you overview the day, you can see that your roles and goals provide a natural prioritization that grows out of your innate sense of balance. It is a softer, more right-brain prioritization that ultimately comes out of your sense of personal mission.

—STEPHEN R. COVEY, *The 7 Habits of Highly Effective People*

Today we spend more time on our therapists' couch than on our own two feet. Psychotherapists are now the skycaps of our emotional baggage, except they're getting $150 tips and putting our bags on a flight that never seems to land. We have 12-stepped over the line, people.

—DENNIS MILLER

M ost people are so busy knocking themselves out trying to do everything they think they **should do**, they never get around to what they **want to do**.

—KATHLEEN WINDSOR

STRESS

is an ignorant state.

It believes that everything is an emergency.

—NATALIE GOLDBERG

Happy people

seem to live less frenetically. They have more time

in their lives. They live more in the moment. This

happiness is available to all of us.

—STEPHEN RECHTSCHAFFEN

What activities,

roles or aspects of your life

bring you the most

joy and accomplishment?

What gives you the most grief?

When we are "mindful", we meet the moment completely, without being driven by our unconscious prejudices, assumptions, and conditioning. In this way, every moment of mindfulness becomes a moment of freedom that liberates us from mindless habits. That is why it is the cornerstone for creating balance in our lives.

—JOEL LEVEY AND MICHELLE LEVEY

If you are willing to learn your lessons gently, they patiently await you in countless ways. Today, try to listen to the wisdom of children; accept the loving kindness of a friend; reach out to those in need; ask a colleague for advice; act on your intuition; laugh at your foibles and frailties and accept them with love; rediscover the surprising healing power of spontaneity; expect the best of every day; **realize what a wonderful life you're living**—sooner rather than later.

—SARAH BAN BREATHNACH

What indications are you receiving that your life is out of balance?

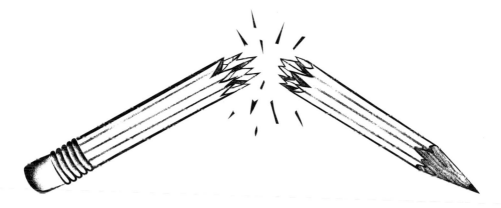

6 SECRETS for an Incredibly Balanced Life

Build a super-efficient support network. Delegate what you can, and get help where needed. You can't do everything by yourself so why even try? The overextended trap is deadly.

Define your relationships pronto. Which ones are your priorities? Which ones can withstand being on the backburner? Start easing out of relationships or obligations which are not mutually supportive and add more stress to your life.

Jump into life big time. That doesn't mean rushing around from one thing to the next. Take a yoga class. Learn to spin. Take up qigong or tae-bo. Find an activity you love to maintain a healthy sense of balance. The perks will pay off.

Learn how to go with the flow. Stuff happens so be resilient and roll with the changes. There's no use being hard on yourself over things out of your control. Realize it and move on.

Make time for yourself a priority. Create some alone time to help you develop a stronger, deeper more precious relationship with yourself. Meditate, read, listen to music, take a long bath. Just remember to leave the guilt behind and bliss out.

Work is work. Play is play. Both are necessary but keep them separate. Don't take work with you on vacation. Or worse, don't forgo time off because you're too busy. Remember the old "I wish I had spent more time at the office" epitaph. Enough said.

Balance, properly understood, is a cyclic dance of learning, meeting challenges,

more learning, more accomplishments. At each step, you are able to bring a

higher order of understanding to handle a greater degree of complexity in the

challenge. Now, how long do you think these cycles of development and

accomplishments go on? Forever. **Lifelong learning is a way of life,** not just a nice idea.

—JOEL LEVEY AND MICHELLE LEVEY

Not living a balanced life takes its toll. Please have the exact change.

ACTION

Only when you have the self-awareness to reexamine your program—and the imagination and conscience to create a new, unique, principle-centered program to which you can say "yes"—only then will you have sufficient independent will to say "no" with a genuine smile, to the unimportant.

—STEPHEN R. COVEY, *The 7 Habits of Highly Effective People*

Live your life

so that your children can tell their children that you not

only stand for something wonderful—you acted upon it.

—DAN ZADRA

Make a commitment to yourself to discover meaningful and effective action you can take to contribute to and support the healing and transformation in the world. Look around you to see some of the problems and issues in your immediate environment or out in your community.

—SHAKTI GAWAIN

An idea

not coupled with action
will never get any bigger
than the brain cell it occupied.

—ARNOLD GLASGOW

LOATHING MONDAY is a lame way to spend $\frac{1}{7}$ of your life.

—UNKNOWN

Yes, risk taking is inherently failure-prone. Otherwise, it would be called sure-thing-taking.

—TIM MCMAHON

There are so many things that we wish we had done yesterday, so few that we feel like doing today.

—MIGNON MCLAUGHLIN

10 Signs It's Time to Get Moving

1

You never laugh anymore.

2

You're as shaky as a horror movie handcam.

3

Your nickname is "Miss Placed."

4

You're constantly devising a New Plan of the Week.

5

You hear "Lighten up" more than once a day.

6

You whine so much you can't remember the sound of your regular voice.

7

You're not yourself and no one likes the new you.

8

The word "grounded" reminds you of high school.

9

All Talk No Action is your mantra.

10

You've fallen and you can't get up.

Never confuse movement with action.

—ERNEST HEMINGWAY

Life is full of obstacle illusions.

—GRANT FRAZIER

*T*his is a story about four people named Everybody, Somebody, Anybody, and Nobody. There was an important job to be done and Everybody was sure that Somebody would do it. Anybody could have done it, but Nobody did it. Somebody got angry about that because it was Everybody's job. Everybody thought Anybody could do it, but Nobody realized that Everybody wouldn't do it. It ended up that Everybody blamed Somebody when Nobody did what Anyone could have.

—UNKNOWN

WARNING: Dates in calendars are closer than they appear.

EMPOWER

In addition to self-awareness, imagination and conscience, it is independent will that really makes effective self-management possible. Empowerment comes from learning how to use this in the decisions we make every day.

—STEPHEN R. COVEY, *The 7 Habits of Highly Effective People*

In this culture, we are too busy to take the time to tell ourselves the positive messages we need to hear. Isn't it funny how we always seem to find the time to tell ourselves how lonely, ugly, or fat we are? How much we hate ourselves, our jobs, and our mates? Yes, we always seem to have time for the negative. But when it comes to taking five minutes a day to stare in a mirror and repeat a positive message of love and understanding to the universe, well...sorry Charlie—only good-tasting tuna get to treat themselves well.

—BEN STILLER

Paint from your own palette.

If I put my mind to it,
I COULD DO ANYTHING.

I just don't feel like putting

my mind to something. So there.

—ELLEN DEGENERES

Authentic power has its roots in the deepest source of our being.
Authentic power cannot be bought, inherited or hoarded. An
authentically empowered person is incapable of making anyone
or anything a victim. An authentically empowered person is one
who is so strong, so empowered, that the idea of using force
against another is not part of his or her consciousness.

—GARY ZUKAV

How Empowered Are You?

Rate yourself from 1 to 5 (1=very little, 5=very strong)
on the following traits:

✳ When action needs to be taken, you take it yourself.

✳ You learn from bad experiences instead of repeating them over and over.

✳ You take good care of yourself regardless of what's going on in your life.

✳ You expect the best from yourself but when it doesn't happen you get over it.

✳ You laugh at yourself and find humor in exasperating situations.

✳ You're comfortable with yourself. You know you're not perfect but who cares?

✳ You're hip to your mood swings. You know you can't always be "on."

✳ You listen to what others are saying instead of waiting to cut in with your story.

✳ You are able to think of creative solutions to problems and enjoy
the challenge.

✳ You trust your intuition and gut feelings. Your inner psychic is always tuned in.

✳ You can let go of the past. You prefer to live in today with an eye
on the future.

✳ You help others without worrying about getting a payback.

✳ You value your lessons in life instead of going into a full-out "why me" act.

✳ You revel in your uniqueness and wouldn't want to be anyone but you.

SCORING
60–70 Highly efficient machine
50–60 Powered up more than most
40–50 A quart low but doing okay

30–40 You need an overhaul
30 or under You're totaled,
seek help immediately.

Eat like you've just had a heart attack.

Work like your job description is under consideration.

Talk like everyone can overhear what you say.

Live like you're going to have a face-to-face with your Creator every day.

—STEPHEN COVEY

Power can be taken, but not given. The process of the taking is empowerment in itself.

—GLORIA STEINEM

**KNOWING
OTHERS**

is intelligence.

**KNOWING
YOURSELF**

is true wisdom.

**MASTERING
OTHERS**

is strength.

**MASTERING
YOURSELF**

is true power.

—TAO TE CHING

The question isn't who is going to let me; it's

who is going to stop me.

—AYN RAND

About Franklin Covey

Franklin Covey is the world's leading time management and life leadership company. Based on proven principles, our services and products are used by more than 15 million people worldwide. We work with a wide variety of clients, Fortune 500 material, as well as smaller companies, communities, and organizations. You may know us from our world-renowned Franklin Planner or any of our books in the 7 Habits series. By the way, Franklin Covey books have sold over 15 million copies worldwide—over 1½ million each year. But what you may not know about Franklin Covey is we also offer leadership training, motivational workshops, personal coaching, audiotapes and videotapes, and *PRIORITIES* magazine just to name a few.

Let Us Know What You Think

We'd love to hear your suggestions or comments about *Purpose: Focusing on What Matters Most* or any of our Portable 7 Habits books. All seven books in the series will be published in 2000.

www.franklincovey.com/portable7

The Portable 7 Habits
Franklin Covey
MS0733-CK
2200 West Parkway Boulevard
Salt Lake City, Utah 84119-2331 USA

1-800-952-6839
International (801) 229-1333 Fax (801) 229-1233

PERMISSIONS

RECOMMENDED READING

Adrienne, Carol. *The Purpose of Your Life*. Eagle Brook, 1998.

Adrienne, Carol. *The Purpose of Your Life Experiential Guide*. Eagle Brook, 1999.

Bragg, Terry. *31 Days to High Self-Esteem*. Peacemakers, 1997.

Cope, Stephen. *Yoga and the Quest for the True Self*. Bantam, 1999.

Gawain, Shakti. *The Path of Transformation*. Nataraj, 1993.

Levey, Joel, and Michelle Levey. *Living in Balance*. Conari Press, 1998.

Levoy, Gregg. *Callings: Finding and Following an Authentic Life*. Harmony Books, 1997.

Moody, Harry R. *The Five Stages of Soul: Charting the Spiritual Passages That Shape Our Lives*. Anchor Books/Doubleday, 1997.

Patterson, Ella. *1001 Reasons to Think Positive*. Simon & Schuster, 1997.

Salzberg, Sharon, ed. *Voices of Insight*. Shambala, 1999.

Schaef, Anne Wilson. *Living in Process: Basic Truths for Living the Path of the Soul*. Ballantine Wellspring, 1999.

St. James, Elaine. *Living the Simple Life*. Hyperion, 1996.

Tolle, Echart. *The Power of Now*. New World, 1999.

VanZant, Iyanla. *One Day My Soul Just Opened Up*. A Fireside Book, Simon & Schuster, 1998.

Williamson, Marianne. *Enchanted Love*. Simon & Schuster, 1999.

Winston, Stephanie. *Getting Out from Under*. Perseus Books, 1999.

———. *Best Organizing Tips*. A Fireside Book, Simon & Schuster, 1995.

Witting, Chris, Jr. *21 Day Countdown to Success*. Career Press, 1998.

Zukav, Gary. *The Seat of the Soul*. A Fireside Book, Simon & Schuster, 1990.